the light we cannot see

anne casey

PRAISE FOR THE LIGHT WE CANNOT SEE

"Anne Casey's The Light We Cannot *See aches with loveliness even as it warns against humanity's pervasive damage to the environment. Poem after elegant, ecocritical poem showcases Casey's grasp of the environmental crises we have created in the Anthropocene—whether it's the bleaching of the Great Barrier Reef ("Where once she danced"), the Australian wildfires ("This is not a drill"), or the rising ocean levels ("At sea"). But she interweaves each poem with such a profound beauty that we cannot help but to remember that at least with poetry, humans have created something good. This is a work that breaks your heart with its almost elegiac approach to ecology and the Earth—and yet, Casey offers that scintilla of hope that with human change, all is not lost ("Either way, the fact remains"). A wonderful and staggering collection of poetry.*

JC Reilly
Managing Editor of *Atlanta Review*
author of *What Magick May Not Alter*

"Anne Casey's poetry is a revelation. Her work effortlessly moves between the metaphysical and the sensual, the concrete and the lyrical, the inspirational and the earthly. Encountering The Light We Cannot See is to encounter a whole range of human experience evoked with poignancy, poise and grace. It's the sort of work that lodges within and stays vivid long after reading."

John Tague
Managing Editor of *Griffith Review*

"Anne Casey's brilliant new collection of poetry is her best work yet — lyrical, experimental, musical and technically sophisticated. Casey engages passionately with urgent global, local and personal issues, from climate change and the COVID-19 pandemic to exile, motherhood, loss and acceptance. Writing in the tradition of Boland, Heaney and Yeats, she exhibits a mastery of form and subject, crafting beautiful, irrefutable appeals to our emotions, ethics and logic."

Nathanael O'Reilly

Poet, Associate Professor, University of Texas at Arlington,
Author of *(Un)belonging*, *Preparations for Departure* and *Distance*

"There is great humanity in these poems, a willingness to be vulnerable and open to emotion. It is matched by a gift for words, an instinct for what can be said and what can only be implied, alongside a true poet's love of the sound and texture of spoken language, whether pronounced out loud or inwardly towards the mind's attentiveness. Family, grief, death and separation recur across these poems, but so equally do the tactile sensations of being alive in this world. Landscapes and weather-scapes, birds and animals, urban chatter and quiet open spaces abound in these engaging poems that explore life as it unfolds in the ominous 21st Century."

Peter Boyle

Poet, Translator of Poetry, Author of *Enfolded in the Wings of a Great Darkness*,
winner of the NSW Premier's Prize 2020

"In this luminous and searing new collection, Anne Casey invites us into her world of ghosts from the old country rearing up in the new and enthralls us with her evocations and invocations, while planting her uncompromising political, yet beautifully softly-gloved fist, in our hypocrisies. This is a book to carry us through the darkness and guide us to 'the light we cannot yet see' in poems that are modern masterpieces."

Indran Amirthanayagam

Author of *The Migrant States*, Editor of *Beltway Poetry Quarterly*

ABOUT THIS BOOK

the light we cannot see traverses a globe caught in the combined turmoil of the climate crisis, COVID-19 and humanitarian unrest, as seen through the eyes of a mother worried for her children's futures and an exiled daughter struggling with loss and separation from loved ones in her native Ireland. Navigating the path of these apocalyptic spheres and their devastating impacts — including catastrophic bushfires in her adopted homeland of Australia — the poet strives throughout this collection of award-winning poems to connect with our "one persisting challenge — to somehow find our allied humanity". A probing reflection on the human condition, this book leans always towards "the light we cannot yet see, but know lies ahead".

the arts council
an chomhairle ealaíon
funding literature
artscouncil.ie

the light we cannot see

anne casey

salmonpoetry40

Publishing in Ireland Since 1981

Published in 2021 by
Salmon Poetry
Cliffs of Moher, County Clare, Ireland
Website: www.salmonpoetry.com
Email: info@salmonpoetry.com

ISBN 978-1-912561-97-1

Cover Artwork: *Jerome Gardes*
Instagram: @urbex_abandoned_
Web: flickr.com/photos/urbex_abandoned_/

Cover Design & Typesetting: *Siobhán Hutson*

Printed in Ireland by Sprint Print

Salmon Poetry gratefully acknowledges the support of
The Arts Council / An Chomhairle Ealaíon

"Come away, O human child!
To the waters and the wild
With a faery, hand in hand,
For the world's more full of weeping than you can understand."

WILLIAM BUTLER YEATS, *The Stolen Child*

for Jack and Joe

... to the moon and back, to infinity and beyond

Awards and recognition for poems in this book

'Prayer-fish' was awarded 2nd Prize in the *Crosswinds Poetry Contest 2021* (USA).

'Prayer-fish' was Commended in the *Tom Collins Poetry Prize 2020* (Fellowship of Australian Writers, Western Australia).

'Exiled' was longlisted in the *Sunspot Literary Culmination Contest 2020* (USA).

'Constitutional' was shortlisted for the *Allingham Poetry Competition 2020* (Ireland).

'Past the slip' received Honorable Mention in the *Crosswinds Poetry Contest 2020* (USA).

'Calling my mother' was shortlisted for the *Bedford International Writing Competition 2020* (UK).

'For all he gave', 'She Understood' and 'Portrait of a funeral arrangement' were shortlisted for the *2020 ACU Prize for Poetry* (Australia).

'Season of Brigid' was shortlisted for *The Plough Prize 2019* (UK).

'Season of Brigid' was Highly Commended and shortlisted in the *Anthology Poetry Prize 2020* (Ireland).

'Season of Brigid' was longlisted for *The Fish Poetry Prize 2020* (Ireland).

'Season of Brigid' was longlisted for the *Trim Poetry Competition 2021* (Ireland).

'On Monday, i ate three strawberries, a pear, a palmful of sunflower seeds & one nicely ripe banana' was awarded 3rd Prize in the *Poetry Day Ireland Competition 2020*, Royal Victoria Eye and Hospital with support from the Research Foundation and Poetry Ireland.

'Signals by sea' was a Finalist and Commended in the *45th Annual Melbourne Poets Union International Poetry Prize 2019.*

'Signals by sea' was longlisted for *The Plough Prize 2019* (UK).

'Like Hesperus o'er the western sea' was shortlisted for the *Allingham Poetry Competition 2019* (Ireland).

‘Pellucid dreaming’ was longlisted for *Palette Poetry — The Emerging Poet Prize 2020* (USA).

‘Where once she danced’ was awarded 2nd Place and Highly Commended in the *Planet in Peril Poetry Competition* (UK) — a joint initiative by Fly on the Wall Poetry Press; World Wildlife Fund; The Climate Coalition; Dr Michelle Cain (Oxford University); former Derbyshire Poet Laureate, Helen Mort; and wildlife photographer, Emily Gellard.

‘Where once she danced’ was Commended in the *2020 Sutherland Shire Literary Competition* (Australia).

‘Night traps’ was awarded 1st Prize in the *International Proverse Poetry Prize 2020* (Hong Kong).

‘Night traps’ was a Finalist in the *Atlanta Review International Poetry Contest 2020* (USA).

‘Night traps’ was selected as a Semi-Finalist in the *Naugatuck River Review 12th Annual Narrative Poetry Contest* (USA).

‘Night traps’ was longlisted for *The Plough Prize 2019* (UK).

‘Either way, the fact remains’ was awarded 3rd Prize in the *International Proverse Poetry Prize 2019* (Hong Kong).

‘Either way, the fact remains’ was nominated for *The Pushcart Prize 2020* (USA) by *Beltway Poetry Quarterly*.

‘Leaning towards solas’ was shortlisted for the *2019 ACU Prize for Poetry* (Australia).

‘Watching and waiting’ was shortlisted for the *Bestiary of the Night Poetry Competition*, Hedgehog Press (UK).

‘Making up the end’ was longlisted for the *Alice Sinclair Memorial Writing Competition 2020* — Fellowship of Australian Writers, Lake Macquarie, NSW (Australia).

Contents

Prayer-fish

for Rory

i.

I saw a crow catch
        another's ragged black
        wing—conjoined,
spiraling down
towards the carmine
        splay of dying
        light on the horizon.

ii.

Three nights before
        he died,
        we stumbled on
the bundle of
dead possum
        curled on its side,
        as if asleep.

iii.

He didn't look
        as if asleep
        streaming live
from the living
room of your childhood
        home, lying
        stiffly in his casket.

iv.

It feels like sacrilege
        to speak
        of this—like the line
I wrote three nights before:
fearing they may not
        survive the long wait
        till we might arrive.

v.

Waking him
        online through two
        days and nights—
fingers conjoined,
familiar words
        spiraling down
        through decades.

vi.

Swimming
        up out of night's
        black wing, a ripple
of muscle
memory jawing
        ...full of grace
        ...at the hour of our death.

vii.

Small silver minnows
        flounder towards
        the horizon:
prayer-fish flopping
up the numb
        length of tongue
        flutter at stiff lips.

viii.

I caught a black crow:
        one ragged wing
        spiraling in, the rest
splayed against
the wind—over
        the great rent
        in his beautiful field.

ix.

The wrench of this
        reshaped horizon
        where you laboured
shoulder-to-shoulder
over his mighty beech—
        felled by wild winds—
        its breadth half his height.

x.

Your breath laboured
        at this great wrench:
        the length of him
felled alongside
the coffin lid—stiffly
        upright, the dying light
        caught in its brass cross.

xi.

We stumble on
        as if asleep
        all week
floundering against
the splay of dying,
        the numb length
        of living.

xii.

I talk about my mother
        dying, tell you
        It's natural—
silver minnows, lying:
there is nothing
        natural in burying
        your father online.

xiii.

I catch your black
          wing—conjoined
          in the ragged
splay of dying light,
together we spiral
          towards the thin
          carmine line.

Exiled

for Indran

We flew with the wind,
sank our feet deep
        into foreign soil,
        drank thirstily
from the poisoned
springs of these mighty
        nations, worshipped
        at the false altar.

As we look now across
all the tumbled wreckage
        from your displaced
        shore to mine,
might we wonder
how we have come
        to this, to this, to this—
        to this slow folding

-in to this abyss
of our own
        creation: how we had
        failed to mother
Earth, suckled
at the flaccid
        paps of Mammon,
        feasted on the spoiled

flesh of dying
species, fleeced
        by specious
        prophesies—
taken down now
not by those great
        dreaded nuclear warheads
        but by *this*—

this microscopic
Armageddon; still to be human
    is to persist
    even at this
infernal pass,
we will stir
    the will to lean
    into the light.

Constitutional

Together in isolation,
tugged by a small eager
        dog who has waited
        all day—we step out

into the chill spearing
off a contracting
        Antarctic, our silence
        implicit: uncomplicated

by unfamiliarity—
winding through
        the familiar
        neighbourhood

of our marriage.
A murder of sorrows
        arrows out of evening
        branches, scatters

into cobalt overhanging
saffron—screeches
        of late-homing lorikeet,
        lights blinking

on across old stone
ramparts thrusting
        up from the eclipsed
        reserve; sure as

taxes, death stalks us
as we turn for home
        past the tumbledown
        wall that speaks

of grander days—conspiring
in our silence, resisting
        the urge to hurdle
        all the closed borders

between us
and all we left behind
　　　—cocooned half the earth
　　　away—arms that had raised

us embracing empty
air and this complicated
　　　new unfamiliality:
　　　silence swallowing

the unfathomable
prospect they may not
　　　survive the long wait
　　　until we are able to return.

Singularity I

for Buzz

Staring back through *that magnificent desolation*
to this devilled blue globe, one dome suspended in light,
the other obscured by the shadow of where you stood;
immersed as you were in light particles
from long-dead stars, did you wonder
at our seemingly eternal journey,
cycling over and over from light
to dark to light? Reflecting on Earth:
seeing 'home' for the first time in that vast
perspective at once vivid and spectral; this silenced beauty
turning slowly over its own desolate truth:
the enormity of its one persisting challenge—
to somehow find our allied humanity
—a singular planetary alignment
as subtly elusive as one
perfect surface reflection.
As great and bungled.
As necessary as the light
we feed on, as desperate
to repel the dark, over and
over to separate and break us
apart from the spectre of some alternative reality,
time folded in on itself, suspending us in an
other perpetual virtual truth
and the hovering ghosts of
what could have been.

Blessed amongst lunacies

I: A living room in west Clare, Ireland—21 July 1969

Hands grasping at the grey screen, agasp—
my brother's face round and bright
as the moon behind, reflecting back
the blue light, this rock around which I orbited,
magnetically attracted & repelled according to
his mercurial moods.

II: Lake Toba, Sumatra, Indonesia—September 1993

Lake-water oddly blood-warm, viscous
& deathly dark. Floating half-naked on my back
within a lapping galaxy; a slick touch—gasp
& panicked turn into that inky, airless realm,
silent but for a muffled thundering; pivoting,
kicking instinctively for light: guided only by stars;
legs still thrusting when they struck shore—
two black wings thrashing in the cage
of my heart, a bone-sliver poking
through silver-pricked black.

III: A medical facility in Sydney, Australia—November 2004

Over the glowing dome of my bare abdomen,
a mottled landscape laid out in grainy greys.
Gasp—at that alien face looming,
a tiny foot poised against black space.
A giant leap into uncharted territory:
struck by the light of my first son, unadulterated then,
but so often since eclipsed by the fear
of what on Earth we will leave them.

Past the slip

No gulls today—
the stiff breeze phantoms their haunting
calls, warm and peppered with salt, a far cry
from where you and I once walked side by side.

Sand crumbling beneath my feet reveals a stone
worn smooth through the years
since your passing:
no longer

the jolt
of thoughts to call
you—is this how long
it takes to exorcise a well-loved ghost?

I can summon you still, though
you no longer visit unbidden:
stricken remembrance
ever my measure

of love, disarmed
always by where you
would be if no longer living
on in me—the sharp shock of

ground eaten away, feet giving way
to stumble under the
fractured edges.
A tangle

of red
exposed roots
dangling in vacant space—
last in a line of tide-besieged palms.

Caught off-balance, two pied oystercatchers
totter into the swirling backwash,
mirroring each other—
the smaller always

one step behind the other,
crimson beaks plunging into
the ebbing rush, twin probes coming up
empty. I catch your missed expression sometimes

in my own glimpsed reflection; a rush of white lace
swallows my feet and I am cut off at the ankles
until it slips away back out to sea, leaving
only its glistening absence.

Calling my mother

I read somewhere there's a man
in Japan who installed a telephone
to the dead
at the end
of his garden:
for privacy reasons
it is inside a white
phone box with lines
of tiny shiny glass panes
like you might see
on any Tokyo street corner
and a row of characters
I can't make out
etched into the painted wooden trim
around the top.

By all appearances
it has become quite popular—
some ten thousand souls
having made
the pilgrimage
to the little garden
on the outskirts of Otsuchi:
you can get there by high-speed train from Tokyo
and you will find it just north of Dai Chiwari 11;
if you come to Dai Chiwari 12
you have gone too far—
a fact that frankly
leaves me somewhat startled.

Much as I would love
to take the trip to Japan
(due to my appalling sense
of direction, almost certainly
relying on Google Maps
if going all that way)
to visit this man
and see his garden telephone box
for making calls
to the dead—

enfolded now in sleeping
winter trees:
a few buds will start
to appear soon
on the stark cherry branches
standing sentinel in the chill air
carrying a trace of salt
from the Pacific just visible
in the distance.
Much as I would truly love to go
whenever I want
to talk to you,

I just do.
Sometimes out loud:
if I'm in the car on my own, for instance—
as to anyone standing next to me
at the lights,
I might be on Bluetooth.
That nice man in Japan should maybe
invent a mobile version
for people who can't make it over
to his lovely garden
where pink puffs will unfurl
into sunlit air
not too long
from now.
I wonder if he might think
of installing a little seat,
maybe a wooden bench
for people waiting their turn
to use the telephone

to the dead.
Sometimes just in my head:
if the kids are home, for example
and I wouldn't want to spook them
with thoughts
I've finally cracked

or we have ghosts in the house
again
after all we did
to get rid of them
that last time
(Jack aged eighteen months
flapping his chubby arms
above his head frantically
and calling
Peoples.... peoples going up...
Up, up, up
in the sky!)
We wouldn't have minded so much
if we had known one or two
of them personally
and they hadn't made
such a nuisance of themselves.

But mostly,
mostly—I have no need
for telephones
or Bluetooth or satellites,
FaceTime or Snapchat
and even though I can hardly
make out your words
any more,
your answer comes through
loud and clear.
Mostly I have no need for
that lovely shiny white telephone box
for talking to the dead
at the end of the garden
in sight of the Pacific
in the foothills of Otsuchi
linked by train from Tokyo city
because I just
talk to you

by heart—
as I am quite sure
that very kind
man in Japan
would understand
if ever
we were to meet—
even with my hopeless
sense of direction,
without benefit
of GPS coordinates
or even Google Maps,
I will always
find you
there.

For all he gave

In loving memory of Philip Lonergan

In the wake of this unfathomable toppling—
the mighty roar and the swallowing silence—
wind-felled, the length and girth
of that gnarled trunk
now laid out before us,
that great rent left in his beautiful field,

the warm heady pull of earth,
the overwhelming urge to curl up
into that vast gap,
to seek again sure shelter
against a sombre outlook,
to lean again into that hushed strength,
to feel the gentle sway of that steadfast ascent.

How deep those roots
that had buttressed all above—
all those quiet, unassuming labours
that had allowed the rest to flourish—
that soaring crown
and every tiny, much-loved, well-nurtured branch,
each unfurling leaf
and quivering bud
that had been so assuredly held up
to the warming sun.

Being the son he made you,
you will walk out now
into this newly shaped horizon,
and lean into the boundless
prospect of
this *grand, fine day*.

She understood

That we are all one
part blood & bone
to two parts
broken star—

I never understood
her in the moment,
but hindsight is a sage
coach and efficient whip:

why she was late that day,
how it might have sparked
my adolescent ire, that
ever-stokable fire;

those long nights alone in the shop,
bitter winter-dark solitude,
my own aloneness
in the house behind;

how she would often seem
to be only half-listening,
lips moving out of time
with my words;

and the tension over books
never quite balancing;
the endless lists, in case
an intercession was missed;

how she knew pure compassion
runs to no human timeline,
how I missed that she had
dependents other than me;

how they leaned in to her
over that counter
year in, year out,
no matter the weather; how a kind

word or the promise of a novena
        was enough for some,
        under-the-counter
dealings for others—

a rushed parcel pressed into wringing
        hands with a hushed *pay when you can*:
        school shoes, a Communion
dress, community necessities

or Christmas niceties—
        brightly wrapped in an
        anonymous pile because
joy shouldn't stop at any threshold—

but it was her gift
        of foresight that drove her
        to lock the door that day,
that made her late for me:

racing down narrow muddy ruts
        to find him, rope-in-hand—
        his whole life lived in this
house with his own late mother.

Who knew, could have known
        how much she understood
        how we need less
than we believe;

how we can survive
        more than we realise;
        how we are all part
-broken;

how it was only as her blood
        & bone broke down, I understood
        how she had always been more
than two parts star.

Portrait of a funeral arrangement

for Denise

Dark stars pierce the luminous heart—
a shrouded mouth fallen open,
a delicate central cross.

        Daubs of captured sunlight
        loll among the upright
        congregated throng.

Burdened others cast out
and down; a huddled cluster
bows off to one side.

        Each with green wings
        flung upwards—as if
        in silent supplication.

Swanlike, cheek to cheek,
a pair intertwine at the neck—
tied for the span of their brief life.

        Your spray of luminous hearted kindness
        to pierce the dark star
        of our grief.

I

i
id
ide
idea
ideate
ideology
ideologue
~~ideal~~

ii

in my native
tongue, i
is topless: it's lost
its head—a lopped
chıcken or dog
-matıc, runnıng
mındless, *wıld*

iii

in my
native tongue,
i is
sometimes topped with a *fada* [i.e. 'long'] soundíng a sílent
scr[*eee*]am—as ín bean sí [banshee: 'woman spírít'] emíttíng hígh pítched shríeks

iv

is what i think is needed in our [sk]in-deep
society—a transfusion of truth wouldn't go amiss
in place of this iphone ipad ipod iwatch itv
in[s]ane existence where the i:eyes have it...
blïnking döts ïn the sky, ïn the walls,
on the ceïlïng, vïa satellïte & sïrï or alex[ï]
& strangers can link to conversations
you've had in the [quasi¿] privacy of your
very own mani[in]fested ïclouded home

ic [*sic*]

is what i'd intimate is missing in this in[v]erted
semi-[un]conscious, icecap-melting, species-oblit[era]ting
p[last]ic-proliferating, media-misap[prop]riating, ideate-[in]filtrating
p[rot]ectïonïst state where independent id is ımpaıred,
Gaia's spirit is shríekíng & ic: to *care intensively* is
the impasse between i-centric conservation &
an[nıhıl]ation

Season of Brigid

Rasp of ground sandstone underfoot
snap and crackle of grass leaves
sticks earth desert -ified
as
human -kind
-ness as a universal
common sense
on this invert -ed soil
its milk already spilt

in this fall of fire here
where even our reversed seasons
have been upturned of late
who will walk us safe over coals
breathe
us through black
plum -age
tender us through sacrificial flame

who will temper my sons
for the season ahead
douse brittle limbs whet
bone- dry edges

keen
before the heat
of the nearing fray

if i shed my cloth -es shred my
finger -tips to the quick on the
splinter -ed blades of these
desiccated grass- lands
reforge
myself in your image
if i pierce my
breast with char -red
iron bark

hang me from hazel branch down by
your sacred spring
will you come then
Brigid
of old will you come then
Bríd, protector of my native land will you
come then will you will you come

All the beautiful outcasts

Stirring early to become unwitting witness
to this illicit marvel in that last gasp of intense
green (the wrong shade for the Council elite).
In between thundering freeways and sprawling
dwellings, not far from the mystery-shrouded new metro,
the unwanted tunnel that will swallow our remaining
respite of ragtag, untouched bushland—a stone's throw from
the dank shelf, a chink in the cliff where Lawson *stretched*
after sessions at the Crows Nest hotel, exchanging spontaneous
verse for a drink—is where wonder struck me post-sunrise: a flash
of flame-bright fur, a swathe of white. Undulating, sundrenched,
two entranced, entrancing fox-mates frolicking, unconscious
of anything but early warmth and each other; unmistakeable rapture
lit by the first fingers of the new day pressing between late summer's
laden branches—soaring trees classified as weeds, so easily condemned—
as easily as these magnificent, misplaced creatures. And later,
tramping past the fox bait warning signs, grief striking as
acutely as horror at the impending loss of them, and
of this vigorous corridor, alive now with spearing
lorikeets, a dive-bombing wattle-bird,
cheeks flashing red in the dead
heat where cicadas catch on, strike
up. And in all that bright, beautiful
bewitching tumult, loss suddenly
swallows me wholly
into silence. All this
flourishing
exuberance, vibrant
as those two dawn-lit outlaws;
all this precious pulsing life:
as vivid and dauntless,
as utterly unsuspecting
of their looming fate
as you had been.

A terrible beauty

"In the casual comedy;
He, too, has been changed in his turn,
Transformed utterly:
A terrible beauty is born."

—'Easter, 1916' by William Butler Yeats

Breathing the same
cubic centimetres of air—
his navy eyes holding
mine and mysteries
I will never fathom—
two sentient beings
regarding each other
through a flimsy metal screen.

Just weeks ago,
I might have suffocated him
without a second glance,
this extraordinary creature
now keeping me
entirely entranced.
Master of hidden microcosms,
unexpected spellbinder—

before he turns
back to his communal duties,
spitting and piling
to conjure this structure
so uncannily like a bone
-white copy of a COVID-19 molecule
and I am abandoned once more
to my isolation

and the faint hum
of mud wasps spitting, piling.

On Monday, i ate
three
strawberries,
a pear,
a palmful
of sunflower
seeds &
one
nicely
ripe
banana

the next day,
i ate nothing at all:
i just curled up in a sunny
corner of the veranda & waited
—when my saliva had thickened
to a pearly gloop, i probed it out
from under my tongue: slowly, slow
-ly allowing it to dry as it met the air:
to form a thread that drifted almost
invisible against the early afternoon
sun & starting at the very backs of my
heels i slowly wove those soft billowy
folds around and around from sole
to crown, a semi-translucent worm
-like pouch: i am in here now, warm
& cushioned from outside sounds,
my skin softening within its silken
sheath, cells melding: all of the
holding in me seeping away
until one day when the
world has settled
back on its axis
and the time
is right to re
-emerge

Antipodean interlude

Thrilled shrieks
pierce still blue
afternoon—
    a party in the garden:
    saffron, crimson,
    emerald slivers

swirl from overhanging
branches as
lorikeets cluster
    to feast on
    teeming liquid
    -ambar seed pods and,

embracing these welcome
minutes' distraction
from distancing measures,
    calls from 'home'
    half a world away—
    a third family member

lost to this
silently creeping curse,
I spread wide my arms,
    stretch heart skyward,
    breathe deeply under
    overarching boughs

and open my eyes
to a small universe
of grey-brown spheres
    gently swaying
    midst the frenzied
    feeding,

each one so like
a tiny spiky
Death Star—
    a perfect
    wooden replica
    of a COVID-19 cell.

One minute to midnight

We
check // her
temper at ure at reg ular
inter vals, alrea dy knOw ing the
ans wer // our fell ed be aut y loll s
in fever ish d reams // e ach b r e a th a lab our:
her l un gs in flame d // all her art eries slOw ly
c logging // cutt ing of f her legs has not s av ed her:
she is s O t ired no w // e ach palp it at ion of her he art
a suffer an ce: she ach es ever y w here for her l o s t
l im bs, l im ply gr ieving her be love d dead // we check
her temper at ure at reg ul ar in ter vals // alrea dy
kn Ow ing the ans we r: an other two de gr ees & she's
coo ked: cat as trophi c c ell ul ar de c ay // a cute r
esp ira tor y di stre ss cO me s ne xt, ent ire spec
ies annihil at ion // Gaia is blee ding fr
O m h e r e y e s // fr Om in s ide:
f r O m O ur h and s // we' re h e r
k ill er st (r)
a i n

The BBC reports

for the first time
in history, manmade
materials now outweigh
all life on Earth.

I am a child of wind and rain,
stone and bog, stratified silt slipping
slowly into relentless seas,
too long gone now from the elements
that shaped me—too far
from my childhood shore—these bones
throb for home, to distance
themselves from decades
of these insatiable cliffs
of glaring glass and
crushing concrete—
floors and walls
consuming all
the wildness
that once made us.

The rain here speaks
the same language
as my own
although it falls
on altogether
foreign
terrain.

We have lost our way
of hearing
its words.

Exhibit A.

for Jack

I don't like zoos, but don't want
the zoo to feed the animals
        to each other—
        as some say may
happen when
funds run dry.

I don't like zoos—caged
animals make me restless,
        my conscience pacing
        the length of each fence
as I take my kids
to help feed the animals.

I don't like zoos, but the tufts
fluttering above the baby giraffe's soaring
        forehead muster a small smile
        and I now see how a zebra might
be taken down by a tiger—that august
magnificence holding me

entirely magnetised
until I am pulled away
        to gawk at the meerkat
        standing high on his hind legs:
ramrod back, head periscoping
to take in his doting

observers. I don't like zoos
as a swing of gibbon, a swoop of
        interloping cockatoos,
        a nuzzle of spoonbill, roll
and tumble of young chimp,
a nestle of fennec fox,

a stalk of red panda,
a lilac flash of fairy
        penguins elbowing past,
        a cheeky splash of seals
stir small waves
of panic as—I really don't want

the zoo to feed the animals
to each other, but it's Mr Hobbs
 who totally flips
 my mind, pacing faster
than my guilt—Mr Hobbs
the sun bear who still

suffers from anxiety
more than twenty years since
 he was saved from the food trade,
 Mr Hobbs whose golden face
and wild amber eyes fail to hide
the darkness behind:

fourteen thousand of his kind
caged and milked for bile—
 this smallest and rarest of bears
 who just now sits up high
having found some slight
glob of honey secreted

in a log nearby—
this shy, bright boy with
 his *heart of the sun*
 turned conservation ambassador,
like the once-wild tigers fighting
palm oil driving native

rainforest decline
from their cage confines,
 the corroboree frogs
 with their loud battle stripes—
saved from extinction
to be conscripted

against their species' plight-
so, though I don't
 like zoos,
 where else
might we see them
in a while?

Signals by sea

for Dad

My father's watery brown eyes skim the horizon
for signs of distress: island to headland and back again—
a lifelong protectorship this former trawler captain will
not abandon in his eighty-second summer as he worries out
the riddle of the red sands washing in on the outlying headland,
frets over the rusty truck piled high with crates of she-crabs
in the middle of breeding season, ferrying away their kind's future
nestling in the red spawn within their chestnut shells—reckless pillage

still riling though he is long-retired. My younger son stands tall,
a small crab scrabbling, between his index and thumb: he has turned
a rock and caught the first of many to be sized up and released as I had done
over and over at his age. Later he will capture a mottled brown fish in his bare hands,
to watch it swim away as we wend our way over this shoreline that sustained our forebears
through generations out of memory—a transfusion of ocean flushing out old truths:
the pulsing thrum of everything existing in equilibrium, *earth, sky, sea*; startling
then at the alien landscape laid out inside the inner reef—tawny

blobs round as over-sized dinner-plates, faces akin to grandfather
clocks counting down the sky, tentacles swung like stinging pendulums
across the silver sand: some amongst their hundreds still plump and pulsing, some sunken

around apricot mounds of innards, countless entirely dried out to burnished sundial imprints,
deliquescing like some Doomsday-Clock-Dali-esque renaissance—sizes and species
I have never seen here in all my years. We plough through over the headland
to the flattened strand where once I leapt from thorn-topped sand-dunes
daredevilling with cousins from ridges three and more times

our heights to roll and land in soft piles of windblown sand,
my inner lip still silvered witness to a misstep, hitting so hard
my knees sent front teeth through bunched gum. Along the half mile, half
as wide, the land now levelled and scooped out by newcomer winter storms
defying living reminiscence, to find the ragged scar of clashing sand jagging in,
a curious salmon overlaying native silver all along the tideline, as my father had
described—a taint I saw reflected after as we journeyed to our new 'home', hovering for
hours over the frayed rectangles of henna, sepia, umber and bare ochre carved out from sea

to shining sea—signs of distress echoed as we soared closer over red gums slated
for destruction (to make way for a new motorway) whose wounds bleed ruddy
as the thick stream that had slicked my chin at ten. I touch their
crusted russet cuts sometimes as I walk the parting sea
of breeze-whispering leaves that always seems to sing to me
of my western ocean home, so far now from where we have drifted
for over an hour through city traffic to be spewed out onto the red-brick path
to our front door, distance from country marked out once more by an amber trail.

Like Hesperus o'er the western sea

"To see a babe before his mother's door,/Sharing his morning's meal/ with the green and golden basilisk /That comes to lick his feet."

—Percy Bysshe Shelley, *Queen Mab*

Spearing out of steel-grey water,
it lands on the blue-black reef-tip,
with a flick of its slick head,
transfixing us—three generations rapt
in the parked hatchback—
staring through silver darts stabbing
at the fogged-up glass.

Islanded by a rising tide,
the cormorant flips a thick
inky streak from its hooked beak,
uncoiling mid-air to be caught,
hocked, half-swallowed—
landing in a loop before our eyes
—bulging

inside its gasping windpipe.
We look on astonished as eel
and seabird each wrestle for survival.
Unable to lift back
into the darkening skies,
the cormorant flounders
against the flooding current—

as my father, sons
and I watch
from our wind-rocked box
down by that ravaged strand
alongside our ancestral lands, where
last winter's superstorms cut deep
into coastal flanks.

Mulling over my two
wide-eyed boys
        taking in this mortal struggle,
        I stare down my own basilisk:
in this beleaguered world,
I fear what needle-teethed eel
we'll force them to swallow.

Pellucid dreaming

i:

To be as complete as the greater part   of your self
        composed.

To trust without knowing   when to hang on
        how to let   go.

To have the ability to resist   gravity
        in states   out of quo.

To be divisible   by light
        one part visible to two   invisible.

ii:

More than two thirds of you
        already knows   the way.

You have mostly existed   outside
        of time—

body unto body: disembodied,
        soaring out of dust   into earth,

from dirt to root to stem
        to leaf: remaking light to feed.

iii:

To carry, baptise, flourish   to harbour
        new life,

to realise
        we are all made   of pieces   of each other—

frozen out of time,   through space—
        the greater part   of us

has gazed past   all that is known,
        beyond   the heavens themselves.

Hold fast to dreams

How you *astonish a mean world with your acts of kindness*—
repurposing our wreckage, to swallow an oil rig or a bicycle,
a ship, a sunken chest—your indiscriminate accretion
of abundant goodness over manufactured ruin,
inching forward to harbour a waterlogged rainforest:
lustrous treasure unfolding so close to the sun-slick surface.

Born at the dawn of Ordovician
time, how you embrace intricate multiplicities—
tiny lavish-hearted conservationist, tireless labourer,
magnanimous host: from such small quarter
to house, to home one quarter
of Neptune's herds.

Each delicate tendril pressed
to service—to sculpt your hardy battlements
that bear the brunt of Poseidon's rage, warding off waves,
how you shelter and sustain imperiled island domains.
Embattled, unsung, nocturnal bloomer—how you
take your cue from the moon

to launch upon our *sea of troubles*
a glimmering burst, a pulsing universe of glittering stars,
to whisper: *shut your eyes and see*—each one a freely-given gift,
embryo of hope: if we dare
to dream.

Encomium *boronia granitica*

You purple-tongue parched
air, dust-sieve to
sip afterbirth
of stars.

You tilt: yellow-eye amaranthine
sky, divine
dirt, pious
spoors.

You stem brush
-fire, persist
desert
scree.

You riff idle breeze,
(fi)lament
lyrebird
shrieks.

You grief black
-throated finch,
sorrow wallum
frog.

You ossuary bettong, paradise
parrot, rat-roo, hopping
-mouse, dusky
flying-fox.

You rapture absence,
perfume silence,
perfect solitude,
ghost dark.

You shrine dayfrog,
eastern quoll, white
-footed tree
-rat.

You catacomb wombat,
dunnart, grass
-wren, leaf
-nosed bat.

You who have Lazarused
through planet
-ary shifts—
all of this

yet—how to resist blind
loons thick-fisting
for fools'
gold.

O *diolcogaster claritibia Alberta*

O
to be so useful—
dark-armoured,
chrome-lamped,
stork-limbed,
four-winged.

O
field-faerie—
opal-infused,
felt-antlered
supplanter,
mother of pearls.

O
to fit inside this O—
to orchestrate
delicate harmonies,
O winnower of
mothly thieves.

O
to pierce
plump wriggling flesh,
plant maggots
to writhe Medusa-like,
cannibalise from inside.

We too could be so
translucently beautiful, yet
instead choose to breach Mother
Earth's delicate shell,
laying the seeds
to feed

on our own
future young.

At sea

for Anne

Brine rises, whetted as memories in my sandbagged lungs—
plastic-scrap semi-sunk in a spring tide, ragged and limp, as hard to inflate.

I came from the sea, a distant shore pummelled even then—
beaches these days reshaped by each season, squalls outside living recollection.

Seawater pillowed my children before they were born—
blood-warm as the currents swarming to nurture the Crown of Thorns, they thrived into life.

Wave-surges swell on the storm-ravaged islands of my consciousness—
welling like water-winged infants, as vulnerable to submersion; I still worry they'll drown.

My body grows nodules virulent as invaders engulfing virile organs—
once plump and vigorous as coral polyps, my cells too, pulse with petrochemicals.

My temperature rises with each falling number—
two thousand species, two thousand metres deep, two thousand kilometres wide.

My heart sinks—
faster than the five hundred billion plastic bags we use each year.

My vision clouds—
murky as forty per cent of the world's ocean surface obscured in manmade debris.

But, small and bright as spawn-clouds blooming—
white, gold, coral, the young surfacing, shine through seeking truth:

our budding hope.

Where once she danced

for Janet

Beyond the sleepy dapplings of the mangroves,
trailing lazy limbs into the drowsing waves—
          across the turquoise crests of placid currents
          that lap up to the gently sloping shore—

out past the breakers idly frothing,
beneath the rolling drifts of whitecap spray:
          once I saw her dance, her head encircled brightly
          in blooming rubicund and blazing saffron stars—

tresses dressed with every hue there budding,
ribbons streaming emerald and vivid sapphire-blue,
          peacock-feathered tendrils trailed behind her—
          a giant clam gasped deep and wide with awe;

humpback whale came to slowly drift above her—
their voices joined the wind to sing her praise;
          seals paused to frolic in her swirlings,
          a Maori wrasse gliding past took his fill,

and later as the evening stretched and lingered—
slow to let the day slip to the sea,
          the sun came slanting through that glassy window
          to spread a crimson blanket for her sleep;

leaping with first light came the dugongs
and dolphins circling idly by her side,
          dragon-fish nimbly flitting through her fingers,
          Neptune's Cup Sponge brushing past her toes

as clownfish coaxed a path around her shoulders
where her braids were twined with amber
          and with rose; turtles grazed on grassy rolling
          borders, porcupine ray rippling in the flats;

ribboned pipefish nibbled at the treats she offered,
mantis shrimp and krill came picking at the crumbs
    in her garden suffuse with every colour,
    bottlebrush bordered staghorn skirting ferns,

but storms came to dash her radiant features—
her gorgeous tresses have all turned white with woe,
    her feathered boas are falling all around her—
    blossoms fading from magenta, fuchsia, gold;

angelfish in anguish bow their heads down,
swimming hard against a swiftly rising tide—
    she is drowning in a sea awash with cobalt,
    deadly metals fill the channels where she breathes;

her lovely limbs are shackled down with plastics,
her lungs are laced with deadly manganese—
    a crown of thorns to pierce her pretty head,
    a bed of sludge to lull her in her dreams;

her cherished creatures perish all around her—
in the clutch of slowly simmering seas
    where once beyond the dapplings of the mangroves,
    beneath the drowsing waves and turquoise crests,

way out past the breakers idly frothing,
I saw her dance, her head encircled brightly
    in blooming rubicund and blazing saffron stars—
    tresses dressed with every hue there budding,

        ribbons streaming emerald and vivid sapphire-blue.

Night traps

for Joe

At twelve, he's too old to believe
in monsters I think as we huddle,
        faces swarming with swirling
        colours from his bedside lamp, medusas
undulating in watery obscurity, fear clouding
his ordinary radiance   and my heart

a snared hummingbird: the unanswered
question my bright-eyed boy flounders around
        always in darkness—shut down to
        his daylight wonder: rushing   to greet
the leaf-tailed gecko (long-time resident behind
our outdoor couch) which recently produced a tiny replica,

the brush turkey tightrope-strutting
the length of the fence, wide-eyed possums
        glinting from dusky branches as his teenage brother
        grumbles past to sort trash   and practice his cynicism
What's the point? My teacher says they don't
get recycled anyway…   trust crumbling   like the dust

of so many cicada skins so eagerly plucked
from nearby swamp oaks—spectral   sentinels,
        those exoskeleton twins left to witness the fading
        Please don't bulldoze this   appeals falling
on deaf ears—a whole forest nobody hears
destined to be carted off in mulching trucks

under orders of our neighbour, the State Premier,
who visited his school to shake hands
        before writing off   our precious bushland—
        where once he bobbed   bound to my heart,
cooing as we ducked a troupe
of black cockatoos swooping through,

toddled to the counting of water dragons,
ran to track that elusive rock   wallaby,
        raced to chase white tiger
        moths; stopped to probe bandicoot
droppings   (with a stick); chewed over   the albino galah,
anaemic anomaly amidst its pink flock—all signed off

to make way for a new   motorway
with its undercover proviso: a thirty-year *no*
        public transport clause—artificial sweetener
        for behind-the-scenes dealers, while it seems
around us the whole world is burning   or drowning
as we flail   against federal plans pledging certain

destruction to Earth's largest living structure—
where at three he paddled off, lost   in wonder
        and each year since, we've gurgled together
        through butterfly shoals, skirting bug   eyed
reef sharks, jump-scaring at feinting parrotfish,
gaping through fogging goggles at giant clams and   brain

corals where we swam shoulder-to-shoulder
with an ancient turtle, before
        bubbling back up to the surface like
        his   unanswerable question:
Where will they go Mum,   when
all the trees are gone? And the reef?

A thousand tiny wings
skip a beat as I bend
        to kiss his pillowed cheek
        wanting so much   to lie
to him that the monsters scratching
at his windows   aren't real.

Watching and waiting

for Deb

If you listen carefully   you can hear them
whispering amongst themselves   about us   and how we   came to be.

I found one   in our garage once   almost luminous white   with the faintest hint
of ghostly green   lurking behind a cardboard box   of forgotten important things.

It had made its way   from the far end   of the garden
all the way under the house   and up through   the concrete floor,

sitting there in the semi-dark   all fragile and inert   unless you strained right up close
to those anaemic waxy tendrils   the fine white hairs   vibrating with the creed:

> *"Long, long ago when Mother Earth was free—*
> *Before the first Human was made, all the Trees lived in harmony*
> *With every Creature under Father Sky. All the world existed in perfect balance—*
>
> *But one day Small Grey Rabbit stopped to graze*
> *Near Mountain Stream. Weeping Willow watched Small Grey Rabbit*
> *Bounding about, her tiny feet free to take her wherever her little heart pleased.*

Weeping Willow shook with jealous desire
To pull his feet from the restraining soil. A branch broke off and fell to Earth—
Crushing Small Grey Rabbit—her blood staining the soil at Weeping Willow's feet.

Willow greedily drank the spilled blood.
Father Sky darkened and Great Wind blew, uprooting Weeping Willow
With a mighty screech that foretold Willow would forevermore walk on two legs;

All his children would be born from blood;
They would no longer be nourished by Father Sky
Or nestle in Mother Earth's warm embrace. From that day forward,

Willow and his progeny were condemned
To roam the earth, struggling to survive—until
They had returned every last drop of plundered blood."

If you listen carefully   you can hear them
whispering amongst themselves   about us   and how we'll   meet our end.

That's right   the trees have our number
peering in a window   scratching at a roof   they understand

justice is a waiting game.

In the public interest

A single blue-black blot floats in an eggshell sky
as I pull the blinds, eyes catching a russet streak
        disappearing into the scrub. Outlaw into outlaw—
        a lone fox vanishing into condemned bushland—
our precious reserve exempt from protection,
over-ridden by State law provisions: to *provide*
        for the burgeoning urban population, a new tunnel
        which (for unclear reasons) will exclude public transport.

A single blue-black blot floats on my eggshell
shoulder after cries in the blue-black night,
        waking to the clatter and bang—storming
        uniforms, blue-black in the harsh flash
of overhead fluorescents, prodded by
rifle-butts from crowded bunks: *Papers, papers!*
        Recognising machine-guns without knowing how
        or why, I fear the need for small white lies.

A single blue-black blot floats in my eggshell
palm as I give the well-rehearsed answer,
        my non-birthright passport held until
        my occupation is cross-checked, passes muster.
Communications worker and I am waved on
into the waiting throng. Another barrier crossed,
        knowing just by owning my work, I can be
        deemed wrong, on my return to *safer* soil.

A single blue-black blot floats on an eggshell form:
this small seal of *approval* as my counterpart pulls
        the blinds, to view the warrant—privacy disappearing
        into thin air: a lone trust, long-held, vanishing in this dawn
police raid on rights to know, investigate, report—privileges
over-ridden, withheld by sweeping new federal laws:
        domicile overturned for reporting on secret talks
        to probe our text messages, emails, bank records.

A single blue-black dot blinks in the eggshell sky
as we pull the blinds: invisible to the naked eye.

This is not a drill

Mom and daughter Robinson take off
their gas-masks as they enter the shop.
The air looks murky outside, everything
suspended in blue haze. Experts say Earth
has been hit by a meteorite (or so we think
so far). The impact was like an atomic bomb.
Vast areas engulfed in flames. Many people
have died. Or lost their homes. The military
have been deployed. Some say it is
the Apocalypse. There is no immediate
solution in sight. The nightmare continues.
This is a flashback scene. The Robinsons
are *Lost in Space* now. This is fiction.

The fire alarm goes off as I enter the shop.
Outside in the open-air mall a siren sounds
over and over. Over a loudspeaker a tinny
voice advises us that the fire alarm
has been activated. We are instructed
to stand by for further instructions.
After ten ear-splitting minutes,
no further instructions are issued. No one
has stood by, much less slowed, in their hot
pursuit of bargains in the January sales.
The air quality app on my phone bleeps
a warning. It is *hazardous to be outside*,
breathing the suspended blue haze
that has swallowed most of Sydney.
We are not wearing gas-masks. My lungs are
burning. Experts say the wild bushfires
ravaging this country are like the impact
of an atomic bomb. Over a million hectares
engulfed in flames. Many people have died.
Or lost their homes. The military have been
deployed. My son says it is the Apocalypse.
Earth is trying to stop us Mum
before all the animals are gone.
There is no immediate solution in sight.
This is not a flashback scene. This is not fiction.

This is today and every other day
in Sydney since early November last year.
Watching and praying for friends
to our north, south and west fighting
to save their homes. Ordinary heroes
everywhere risking their lives. To our east,
the ocean carries smoke four hours' flight
to New Zealand. Navy ships dock
at blaze-besieged beaches to rescue
stranded families from their Christmas
escapes. We are *lost in the space* now
between when this nightmare started
and its unforeseeable end.

5 January 2020, Sydney

After the worst

you start
to notice small
signs of life and realise
    how long you had held
    your breath in their absence:
    kids kicking

ball on a neighbouring street,
a whoop and cahoot—
swoop of cockatoos
    acrobating the electric-wire,
    cicadas splitting air
    and eardrums through a haze

of red gums,
clatter
and scatter of blue
    tongue,
    a flurry of lorikeets
    screeching through arrest you

in the aftermath
of this smoke-choked summer—
almost enough
    to lift
    the smog of loss
    while

our tainted antipodean
atmosphere
circles
    this
    hobbled
    globe.

Either way, the fact remains

There is no way back
Therefore we can no longer hold as irrefutable truth that
Every human heart has sufficient good at its core
That we could muster the collective will necessary to save our precious planet
There is no denying
We are capable of taking the measures necessary for our own survival
To secure the future for us and the almost nine million species around us
We could make the right choices
The fact remains that
Earth cannot repair itself
There is no basis even from advanced satellite findings to show that
Earth and all who dwell on her can survive the impacts of human activities
The greatest scientific minds of our time attest that
The world's largest living structure, the Great Barrier Reef, is on-path to certain destruction
That
Over two thousand species from sea-level to two thousand metres deep are destined to perish
We can no longer support the assertion that
There is always a way—
There is a way to undo the damage we have done—
Allowing that we make every effort to counter global excesses
The impact of human activities is irreversible
Although we may think

That we can take action to fix this
We cannot deny the inevitability
That not one of us can make a difference
Nature cannot heal itself
We can no longer lie to ourselves that
This devastation can be reversed
(Now read each line from the bottom up.)

Out of the mouths of babes

Why do they
name hurricanes
after people Mum?

Because people come swinging
at you out of nowhere, relenting
only to catch you again with their rage.

Because people are all drifts—
capable of enormous cruelty
only to disappear in its wake.

Because things are so often
named after their creators—
look at all we have made for you.

But of course I said
none of those things—
he is only ten

I don't know the reason my love—
let us think of
a good one.

Work of human hands

Beached whales in New Zealand
        remind me of
        vanished babes in Ireland.
The awful magnitude of it all—
        six hundred and fifty innocents
        dying up and down Farewell Spit,
known to locals as Whales Trap—
        an arch of deadly sand,
        a chain of human hands
joined in desperation
        to save the next wave
        from breaching out of safer waters,
beaching on this hostile hook of land—
        black bodies strewn as
        far as the eye can see.

Human hands too that held
        naked pink bodies—
        lost souls too small to struggle
in their own hostile territory,
        darkness immersing them for years:
        eight hundred disappeared
without a sound
        till they were found,
        pulled one by one from
an empty tank full to the brim.

What strange things
        human hands—
        to raise up or hold down,
their power to save or drown.

The light we cannot see

"I am the way into the city of woe, I am the way into eternal pain,
I am the way to go among the lost."

— Dante Alighieri, *The Divine Comedy, Vol. 1 (Inferno), Canto III: The Gate of Hell* (Anthony M. Esolen translation)

I: Journey through Anaplasia: An itinerary of my mother's passing

We surface abruptly
somewhere between
the third and fourth stages,
two hills wailing
in a keening wind,

your tented knees encircled
by an ice -shrill entreaty
'Take the baby!'—
and I, still nursing my own,
am momentarily distracted

by the thought of where he could be.
Your urgency returning me
to the grimness at hand,
I seize your demon child,

cautious to elude its writhing claws,
while you rise, limp as snow-sludge
in your stained nightdress,
your stormed temple and I
forever failing you

as, bound together
by our imperfections,
we arrive at this unwalled border
having already crossed
the *Ninth Circle of Hell.*
Before us is a barren, gravelly terrain
that slashes savagely
at our exposed soles
as we tramp mapless for forty days.

A vinegar-soaked sponge our only sustenance,
silenced
by our sand-slaked tongues
and the horror I cannot keep
from you—

repulsed each time it breaks
away to snuffle and scratch, gnash and suckle—
until, out of the fortieth night,
a jagged cliff looms, unyielding
to any light, and you
deliver it back,
this clacking
undead infant,
which flies

screeching
from my enfeebled grip as you orphan it
in your last vicious ascent
into the darkly swirling mists
beyond my reach.

Trudging back alone
through all the terrains
we had traversed together, light
bleeds out
ahead
across some far-off palms,

where the living are sleeping.

Glancing back to where
you had passed,
I am frozen
in perpetual immotion,
transformed to stone,
shackled
to your darkest hour

in that abominable landscape
where I had abandoned any god
that I had ever known—
until, roused
by a tiny trembling form,
whose hungry cries are sundering
the tumbled
night,

I am dragged upwards
under
a midnight sky
transmogrified,
pierced through
ten thousand times
by empyrean light.

II: Return to Anaplasia: If you are still here, this is not the end

Out of impregnable gloom
looms an all-too familiar terrain—
round hills rolling in
great grey grainy waves,
like some long-dead
lunar sea-bed—

this over-charted
but under-fathomed territory
where the forebears of my female line
lie buried beneath
a blemished legend, this witch's curse
that I had sworn

would make no claim on me.
A fire-red eddy up ahead—
heat signature of my unseen
demons
that had breached
the gap, failing still to fall foul of me—

my bunched gown,
a swathe of blue, dipped in the middle
over this long-ruptured abdomen,
tumbling away between the twin peaks
of my knees

as I rise
above the gnawing edges,
crimson starlets
falling
to earth
beneath my teetering feet—
demi-demons slithering in the shadows
of my tainted footprints—a scarlet trail
writhing serpentine
between
striated
slopes

as I thrust a handful of gold
at the toothless soothsayer,
recompense for reading my future
in the patterns of my blood—

no more useful than the blind shaman,
her eyes gouged out by her own conceit
and unmerited self-belief, two blackened spoons
dangling from her crocheted pocket:
"You must give

one thousand answers
and follow without question",
her hollow sockets scanning page
after yellowed page:
"Like cures like",

she would declare, reaching for jars to sniff
and crush,
smoulder and pulverise the bitter tonics
I would swallow for three years,
my eyes closed to follow her lead—

that meandering path leading us back
to where we had started,
where at last we parted,
I still heavy with my devils
my purse alone made lighter.

Ascending out of memory, I come upon
a crumpled form,
whose rumpled robes and cragged skin
render him as one with the rock
upon which he squats. An ancient rod caught
between
his cracked and sandalled feet dangles a limp line
into a dark crevasse—as from behind
a beatific smile, he cries:
"Beware the prowling lion
that will devour you!"

The hollow scrape
of his hook cuts through the answering growl
from my innards as, for cover,
I reply:
"My father was a fisherman too,
but of a different kind."

Eyeing my clutched middle,
he offers me a ragged scrap
much like a flap of skin:
"Take this and eat it," he says,
but my parched
tongue gags
on its rusty tang
and the bitter aftertaste of human sacrifice.

"Follow me and I
will meet you at the gate. He is the key."
he pleads, the spurned scab
cupped to his left breast.
But I have already moved on—

descending from
that high rocky place
to a frozen lake
where, from her ivory tower, an ice queen
invites me to sign away my life
so that she can hand it back to me;

the pact agreed, she extends to me
two mottled ovules.
Leaning in, I sense a hissing from within
and wince.
"The blue one
will make you shed your skin
for once and forever.
The yellow will make you happy again",
the frigid regent proclaims.

"But I am not unhappy,
only plagued by this unshakable curse", I venture.
"Stupid child. The yellows
are the solution to the blues."
"But what will cure me of the yellow?" I dare to enquire.
"Ah—" she professes, "There is a pill for that too."

Dismissed with a flick of her wrist,
I turn aside, having already realised
that her majesty high on her perch and I,
with my belly in the dirt,
will never see eye to eye.

Through the waylaid midlands,
I skirt a soapbox prophet
spittling from his makeshift pulpit,
spreading wide his tiny hands to take
in a burgeoning sea of tumbleweed
that echoes
his empty words
in a rasping chorus, stirred by heated winds,
still failing to apprehend the false bottom

in his rambunctious arguments—
the more you take away,
the less you have to give.

Tracing a trail of glistening beads,
I come to a meeting
of ways, marked by a beheaded pieta—
still recognisable by its heaped misery.

Here I ponder all the fallen relics
of decaying faiths laying to waste and,
worn down
now from following
those many false tracks,
I lay me down to sleep
with my demons.

Stirring in obscurity—a trick of the dark,
or words inscribed in an ancient circle:
What makes the righteous-minded
believe
they have the one true answer,
when they never care
to hear the question?
I wake
to the shining faces
of my two blindfolded sons
lifting me out of the semi-gloom,
bearing me towards
a waiting form—the only one
to have ever known
all of me, and love me none the less.

And away with us into the light
we cannot yet see, but know lies ahead.

Leaning towards solas

Beneath the soaring spire,
        row upon row flickering
        with the wind at each entry.
Another penitent
to genuflect and join the waiting
        throng tiered like the small white candles
        they would light for a penny each
to wash away their sins.

After the stroke,
        my grandfather's frozen half
        propped against
my grandmother, hands knotted
before the Child of Prague on the mantle.
        Fervent whispers over
        the dipping flame
in a chipped cup.

My mother's tears hissing
        into the tealight
        beneath her parents' picture
—young again, tending
their tea roses; lit from within
        like the crystal beads trembling
        between my mother's wringing fingers—
my gift to her from Rome.

Beneath a soaring eye,
        row upon row drifting
        with the wind at each entry—
another wave
to wash away the aching—
        bobbing like small white candles
        as my sons race in streaming sunlight
after scattering petals for grandma.

Snow day

for Ken

Waking to the wonder
        in my brother's voice,
        his shrill delight
shaking him for once
from his teenage retreat,

I arose to a new world,
        without colour:
        all crystal-white,
magically softened and
glowing at the edges—

drawing us out
        with its silent allure
        to explore
familiar places
rendered strange.

Past the edge of town,
        undisturbed by a soul,
        caught by the urge
to jump a wall and run
full-tilt into its empty embrace:

whump! I had sunk,
        softly held
        in all that whiteness;
cushioned from the world,
I could be there still.

We dragged home
        without a word,
        fun stolen by the cold;
the sudden warmth at the door,
my mother's voice

reluctantly returning me
        to all the colour and clamour
        of humanity
and a pang
at the loss of all that

peace.

Where gulls cry

I could tell you how the whole earth seems to end
at this one place where the land falls
cleanly into a tumultuous thundering—
the relentless roar of furious millennia crashing
iced cobalt against three hundred million years
of vertical bituminous siltstone stubbornness,
all overlaid with a violence of vivid greenness
inconceivable until witnessed, where the sky splits
open above—brewing caliginous charcoal yielding
to an inevitability of iridescence, streaming
shards spearing simmering drizzle-laden mists,
all lit as if from within with an otherworldly luminosity
approximating divinity, a scene so sharp yet ethereal,
surreal, imprinted in a part of self within but apart
that might burst from this pulsing bone-suit, this
shadow-world flesh-mantle sheerly in the act
of reliving that reminiscence. I could tell you
all of that or I could say how much this exiled

soul aches for home.

Hope spell

Gather together and muddle through under a shifting light:

Spray of   ocean on a predawn shore
Tender essence of   slumbering child

Saffron strands   extracted from sunrise
Dewdrops of   first spring leaf-bud

Aroma of   unfurling lotus blossom
Trace of   breeze on sunlit skin

Wisp of   cloud in cerulean sky
Compress of   forest-floor underfoot

Heart of   tree-shrieking lorikeet
Zest of   gatherings past and future

Warm press of   nestling dog
Lavender   distilled from sundown

Sliver of   skylight crescent-moon
Half-a-dash of   shooting star

Wing of   love over a bordered world

A song for all the lost days

for Carolyn

When all the earth is slipping under
nestling covers of never-knowing
in the ever-sleep shadow of this half
-waking-dreaming-time, I will gather
the last sprigs of lavender
from a raven-feathered sunset
and step into the nothing-nowhere
vastness void between.

I will carry a bundle of berries
from the soaring flowering lauraceae,
a fragrant spray of your adored cilantro,
a cluster of red bell peppers bright
as blood-spurts, a clutch of smoke
-infused chipotle full of fire,
a parcel of limes from the wild
prickly-ash fagara, and (to keep

the ghouls at bay) a carafe of ale
mulled from elderberry blends.
I will find you where the tides
of always and unending drift in
to the coast of ever-spanning time:
by the feet of your beloved giant
sequoia, we'll lay out a feast for
all the waking-sleeping souls.

Together we'll unfold
a muslin full of white Columbine,
and walking to the edge
of your great ocean, we'll unwrap
all the light that we can hold:
leaning in, to lift each tender
petal and set it off to swirl up
on the waves of every shore.

Suggestions for living, a cento

After Jessie Lendennie

Lay still, the sounds heard
the beginnings of comfort; feel
the sea on the wind, the fall-falling
of the wave riding the horizon

and the waves recede beyond the cliffs,
beyond the trees; rows upon rows,
filling their long trailing sacks; in the darkness,
the silence at the centre of the wind, the sound of rain.

In the dark, trace a circle around the willow—
time the slowest of movements; fine rain
against thin glass, against hard stones
like so many broken children; grow

into Gypsy, Hobo, a child of rain;
know water as it seeps from sky,
from the heart; know the sharp light of sun
on bottles broken in the street.

The horizon is both this path and
the edge of the sea; and memory
is a fracturing, a breaking of light and dark
with an old dog who knows all the secret places

down the unpaved road to the calm bay;
become part of something sacred—
salmon in a small stream that rolled
down to the beach, going home or starting out.

Believe in past lives; sit and wait
for everyone to come home—
silver dogs in the sea, unhindered,
gazing down the valley to Liscannor, Lahinch

and the bay; walk the stones of Clahane:
romantic Ireland smells of soft wind;
move slowly among ghosts
whose bodies are anywhere

but here; lose place; follow another pack; maybe
take a wrong turn at the edge of the sea
as the last storm leaves again;
lay still, the night moved

past; brush wonder
as a child, fingers
tapping at windows;
reach out, softly moved.

Making up the end

All those nights alone in the dark,
my eyelashes scraping

the pillow turning
to claws sharpening in the dark

as you stood slowly
freezing for twelve hours—six, seven

days a week, fell asleep
on my pillow halfway

through a story you made up
as you went along

just to save me
from myself

and I'd wake you
so you could invent the ending.

It's twelve years since
I held your hand

until it turned
to ice in mine,

all of the breath in me
left with you

and though I could have filled
a valley full

of shed and held-back tears,
I finally realise what saves us

is what makes us up as we go along,
conquers all the monsters—

the toughest and tenderest
substance in the universe,

the light that reaches
to the end

of all the darkness,
breaches every gossamer layer

between where you went to
and I remain.

It's all we can have and hold,
all we can take with us

in the end:
the more we give away,

the more that
comes back—

if only
we choose:

in the end,
it's only love.

Notes

'Singularity': This poem was written for *Giant Steps* anthology (Recent Work Press 2019) to celebrate the 50th anniversary of the Apollo 11 moon landing. The words "that magnificent desolation" are a quote from Apollo 11 crew member, Buzz Aldrin, the second man to set foot on the moon.

'Season of Brigid': Brigid (*Brigit, Bríg or Bríd*) is an ancient Celtic goddess associated with fertility, healing, poetry, fire, wells and smithcraft. Later adopted as the Christian St Brigid, her feast day is celebrated on 1 February (also the pagan festival of *imbolc*), marking the beginning of the northern hemisphere spring. Amongst many traditions associated with Brigid, some surviving to this day, are the hanging of doll-like effigies and distinctive 'X' shaped crosses (hand-woven from grasses, rushes and rags) near wells and doorways as protective talismans; offering of dried fruit oblations; and pouring of milk into earth as libation.

'All the beautiful outcasts': The italicised words are taken from a heritage sign posted adjacent to Henry Lawson Cave in Flat Rock Gully Reserve, Sydney, which commemorates one of Australia's best-loved bush poets.

'Signals by sea': The words "from sea to shining sea" are from the song 'America the Beautiful', written by Katharine Lee Bates in 1893.

'Like Hesperus o'er the western sea': The poem title and epigraph are from Part I of *Queen Mab* by Percy Bysshe Shelley.

'Pellucid dreaming': The human body is made up of more than two thirds water. Every water molecule in our bodies originated in space and has existed in many different places and forms, some dating back to before the dinosaurs. Essential to life, water is held as sacred in cultures the world over.

'Hold fast to dreams':
1. One of nature's great conservationists, coral occupies less than 0.1% of the world's ocean area while providing a home for at least 25% of all the earth's marine species. Under threat from human activities facilitated by the erosion of environmental protection statutes, coral reefs provide essential wave protection to island communities, and harbour vital fish stocks. Coral colonies are known as "rainforests of the ocean".
2. The title and italicised words are quotes: "Hold fast to dreams" (Langston Hughes), "astonish a mean world with your acts of kindness" (Maya Angelou), "sea of troubles" (William Shakespeare) and "shut your eyes and see" (James Joyce).

'Encomium boronia granitica': *Boronia granitica* is an endangered wildflower shrub native to Australia; all of the animal species noted in this poem are indigenous to the same areas as this plant, and are already extinct or endangered.

O diolcogaster claritibia Alberta: *Diolcogaster claritibia Alberta* is a species of parasitoid wasp. Less than two millimetres long, these wasps play an important ecological role in balancing the numbers of plant-eating moths and caterpillars. The wasps lay their eggs inside the caterpillars of moths and butterflies; the wasp hatchlings eat their way out, killing their hosts in the process.

'Where once she danced' is a lament for the Great Barrier Reef, the largest living structure on Earth, which is in dire jeopardy due to the impacts of human activities.

'In the public interest': On 4 June 2019, Australian Federal Police—acting on a warrant granted under the auspices of protecting Australia's national security—raided the home of a journalist who had investigated a leaked plan to allow widespread new government powers to spy on Australian citizens. On 1 July 2020, China passed a new national security law, bringing uncertainty for freedom of the press and broader civilian rights in Hong Kong.

'Work of human hands' remembers the eight hundred infants whose remains were discovered in a septic tank on the grounds of the Tuam Mother and Babies Home in Ireland in 2017. Further information can be found in an article by the author of this collection entitled *Marked women, unmarked graves* which was published in *The Irish Times* in May 2018, available online.

'The light we cannot see':
1. The epigraph is taken from the Anthony M. Esolen translation of *The Divine Comedy* by Dante Alighieri.
2. 'Anaplasia' is a medical term referring to cellular breakdown commonly associated with the late stages of cancer.
3. "The Ninth Circle of Hell" is a reference from *The Divine Comedy* by Dante Alighieri.
4. "Beware the prowling lion that will devour you" is based on the *Bible, New Testament* quote "Your adversary the devil prowls around like a roaring lion, seeking someone to devour" (Peter 5:8).
5. "Take this and eat it" is from the *Bible, New Testament* (Matthew 26:26) and current Catholic mass settings.

'Leaning towards solas': 'Solas' means 'light' in the Irish language.

'Suggestions for living, a cento': This cento is composed entirely of lines and line segments from *Daughter and Other Poems* (Salmon Poetry 2001) and *Walking Here* (Salmon Poetry 2011) by Jessie Lendennie.

Acknowledgments

My heartfelt, eternal gratitude to the amazing people who have supported and encouraged me to believe in my writing dreams—Jessie Lendennie and Siobhán Hutson at Salmon Poetry, my incredible husband and sons, my late mother, my father, Martin Doyle, Ciaran Carty, Ciara Kenny, Consul General Owen Feeney, Gabrielle Carey, Bhuva Narayan, Luka Bloom, Eamonn and Drucilla Wall, Eleanor Hooker, Lliane Clarke, Peter Boyle, Tuka, Nathanael O'Reilly, Indran Amirthanayagam, Hélène Cardona, Denise O'Hagan, Anne Elvey, Ali Whitelock, Deborah Hart, Wendy J Dunn, Harry Hughes, Deirdre Vaughan, Tim Dennehy, Anne Rynne, Shona Blake, Claire Watts, Rochelle J Shapiro, Shane Strange, Paul Munden, Ken and Emma Casey, Amanda Eggleton, Natalie Fu and the entire Lonergan family, to name but a few.

Sincere thanks to the editors of the following publications in which poems from this collection were first published: *Atlanta Review, Tahoma Literary Review, Connecticut River Review, Writing Water* (Red Room Poetry 2020), *Giant Steps* (Recent Work Press 2019), *Crosswinds Poetry Journal,* the *2020 ACU Prize for Poetry* anthology (Australian Catholic University 2020), the *Griffith Review, Westerly Magazine, The Alphabet of Women* project created by Miriam Hechtman, *Noir Nation, Voices of Women* created by Lliane Clarke, *Boyne Berries, Plumwood Mountain: An Australian Journal of Ecopoetry and Ecopoetics, Planet in Peril* (Fly on the Wall 2019), *Poems of Hope and Resilience from the Pandemic* (IFWG Publishing Australia 2021), *Live Encounters, Days of Clear Light* (Salmon Poetry 2021), *Age of Uncertainty* (RMIT University 2021), *Postcards from the Hedge: A Bestiary of the Night Poetry Competition* prize anthology (Hedgehog Press 2019), *Wrong Way Go Back* (Pure Slush 2020), *The Irish Times, From the Ashes* (Maximum Felix Media 2020), *The Darg* (The Poets' Republic 2019), *Mingled Voices 4* (Proverse Publishing 2020), *Mingled Voices 5* (Proverse Publishing 2021), *apt Journal*, the *2019 ACU Prize for Poetry* anthology (Australian Catholic University 2019), *Globalisation* (MMH Press 2021) and *The Irish Times Magazine.*

Thank you to everyone who has purchased, read, and taken the time to respond to my poetry, or indeed poetry anywhere.

Originally from west Clare in Ireland, and living in Sydney, Australia, ANNE CASEY is an award-winning poet and writer, and author of two previous, critically acclaimed poetry collections—*where the lost things go* (Salmon Poetry, 2017) and *out of emptied cups* (Salmon Poetry, 2019). She has worked for 30 years as a journalist, magazine editor, media communications director and legal author. Senior Poetry Editor of *Other Terrain* and *Backstory* literary journals (Swinburne University, Melbourne) from 2017-2020, she serves on numerous literary advisory boards. Anne's writing and poetry are widely published internationally and rank in *The Irish Times* newspaper's Most-Read.

She has won/shortlisted for poetry prizes in Ireland, Northern Ireland, the USA, the UK, Canada, Hong Kong and Australia, including: *the American Writers Review Contest*; *The Plough Prize*; *ACU Prize for Poetry*; *Henry Lawson Poetry Competition*; *Women's National Book Association of USA Poetry Competition*; *25th Annual Melbourne Poets Union International Poetry Competition*; *Hennessy New Irish Writing*; *Cúirt International Poetry Prize*; *Overton Poetry Prize*; *Bedford International Writing Competition*; *Atlanta Review International Poetry Contest*; *Tom Collins Poetry Prize* (Fellowship of Australian Writers, Western Australia); and, *Fellowship of Australian Writers Queensland Literary Competition.*

Anne passionately believes that every poem, like all art, should leave us changed by the experience. Her poems feature internationally in newspapers, magazines, journals, anthologies, broadcasts, podcasts, music albums, stage shows and art exhibitions—*The Irish Poetry Reading Archive* (James Joyce Library, University College Dublin), *The Irish Times, The Canberra Times, Australian Poetry Anthology, Griffith Review, Atlanta Review, Beltway Poetry Quarterly, Tahoma Literary Review, Quiddity, Entropy, apt, The Murmur House, Barzakh* (State University of New York), *DASH* (California State University), *Connecticut River Review, The Stony Thursday Book, FourXFour* (Poetry Northern Ireland), *Westerly Magazine, Cordite Poetry Review, Voices of Women* and *Plumwood Mountain* among many others.

She holds a Law Degree from University College Dublin and qualifications in Media Communications from Dublin Institute of Technology (Technological University Dublin). She is the recipient of an Australian Government Research Training Program Scholarship for her PhD in Creative Writing at the University of Technology Sydney.

Website: anne-casey.com   Social Media: @1annecasey

Credit: David Clare, First Light Photography

salmonpoetry

Cliffs of Moher, County Clare, Ireland

"Like the sea-run Steelhead salmon that thrashes upstream to its spawning ground, then instead of dying, returns to the sea — Salmon Poetry Press brings precious cargo to both Ireland and America in the poetry it publishes, then carries that select work to its readership against incalculable odds."

TESS GALLAGHER

The Salmon Bookshop & Literary Centre

Ennistymon, County Clare, Ireland